Birdwatching.

6" x 9" and 24 Pages of six birds per page (144 birds seen in the UK). Spare pages at the end.

As this is a logbook, you may need a bird identification book for when you get home to be sure. Take a photo of the bird to make this easier.

Birds in the logbook

Accentors	Ducks	Larks	Skimmers
Accipitors	Eagles	Leaf Warblers	Skuas
Albatrosses	Egrets	Long-Tailed Tits	Snipe
American Sparrows	Estrilids	Longclaws	Sparrows
Auks	Falcons	Longspurs	Spoonbills
Avocets	Finches	Martins	Starlings
Babblers	Finfoot	Mockingbirds	Stilts
Barbets	Flamingos	Mousebirds	Storks
Barn Owls	Flycatchers	New World Warblers	Sunbirds
Bearded Tits	Francolins	Nightjars	Swallows
Bee-Eaters	Frigatebirds	Nuthatches	Swans
Bishops	Gallinules	Old World Flycatchers	Swifts
Bitterns	Gannets	Orioles	Terns
Bulbuls	Geese	Osprey	Thick-Knees
Buntings	Godwits	Owls	Thrushes
Bush Warbler	Grebes	Oystercatchers	Tinkerbirds
Bustards	Greenbuls	Parrots	Tits
Buzzards	Grouses	Partridges	Treecreepers
Cardinals	Guineafowl	Pelicans	Tropicbirds
Chats	Gulls	Penduline Tits	Turacos
Cisticolas	Hammerkop	Petrels	Vireos
Coots	Harriers	Pheasants	Vultures
Cormorants	Hawks	Piapacs	Waders
Coucals	Herons	Pigeons	Wagtails
Coursers	Honeyguides	Pipits	Wallcreeper
Crakes	Hoopoes	Plovers	Warblers
Cranes	Hornbills	Pratincoles	Waxwings
Creepers	Ibises	Quail	Weavers
Crows	Icterids	Queleas	Wheatears
Cuckoos	Illadopses	Rails	White-Eyes
Curlews	Indigobirds	Reed Warblers	Whydahs
Daters	Jacana	Rollers	Widowbirds
Dippers	Kingfishers	Sandgrouses	Woodpeckers
Divers	Kinglets	Sandpipers	Wrens
Doves	Kites	Shearwaters	Wrynecks
Drongoes	Lapwings	Shrikes	

Bird Name: Accentors	**Bird Name: Acciptors**
Identified ☐	Identified ☐
Where seen? On the:	Where seen? On the:
Ground ☐ Plant ☐ Bush ☐ Tree ☐	Ground ☐ Plant ☐ Bush ☐ Tree ☐
Flying ☐ Dead ☐	Flying ☐ Dead ☐
Male ☐ Female ☐ Adult ☐ Chick ☐	Male ☐ Female ☐ Adult ☐ Chick ☐
Details:- Date: ___/___/___ **Location: ______________________** **Bird Variant: ____________________**	**Details:- Date: ___/___/___** **Location: ______________________** **Bird Variant: ____________________**
Bird Name: Albatrosses	**Bird Name: American Sparrows**
Identified ☐	Identified ☐
Where seen? On the:	Where seen? On the:
Ground ☐ Plant ☐ Bush ☐ Tree ☐	Ground ☐ Plant ☐ Bush ☐ Tree ☐
Flying ☐ Dead ☐	Flying ☐ Dead ☐
Male ☐ Female ☐ Adult ☐ Chick ☐	Male ☐ Female ☐ Adult ☐ Chick ☐
Details:- Date: ___/___/___ **Location: ______________________** **Bird Variant: ____________________**	**Details:- Date: ___/___/___** **Location: ______________________** **Bird Variant: ____________________**
Bird Name: Auks	**Bird Name: Avocets**
Identified ☐	Identified ☐
Where seen? On the:	Where seen? On the:
Ground ☐ Plant ☐ Bush ☐ Tree ☐	Ground ☐ Plant ☐ Bush ☐ Tree ☐
Flying ☐ Dead ☐	Flying ☐ Dead ☐
Male ☐ Female ☐ Adult ☐ Chick ☐	Male ☐ Female ☐ Adult ☐ Chick ☐
Details:- Date: ___/___/___ **Location: ______________________** **Bird Variant: ____________________**	**Details:- Date: ___/___/___** **Location: ______________________** **Bird Variant: ____________________**

Bird Name: Babblers	**Bird Name: Barbets**
Identified ☐	Identified ☐
Where seen? On the:	Where seen? On the:
Ground ☐ Plant ☐ Bush ☐ Tree ☐	Ground ☐ Plant ☐ Bush ☐ Tree ☐
Flying ☐ Dead ☐	Flying ☐ Dead ☐
Male ☐ Female ☐ Adult ☐ Chick ☐	Male ☐ Female ☐ Adult ☐ Chick ☐
Details:- Date: ___/___/___ **Location:** **_______________ Bird** **Variant: _______________**	**Details:- Date: ___/___/___** **Location: _______________** **Bird Variant: _______________**
Bird Name: Barn Owls	**Bird Name: Bearded Tits**
Identified ☐	Identified ☐
Where seen? On the:	Where seen? On the:
Ground ☐ Plant ☐ Bush ☐ Tree ☐	Ground ☐ Plant ☐ Bush ☐ Tree ☐
Flying ☐ Dead ☐	Flying ☐ Dead ☐
Male ☐ Female ☐ Adult ☐ Chick ☐	Male ☐ Female ☐ Adult ☐ Chick ☐
Details:- Date: ___/___/___ **Location:** **_______________ Bird** **Variant: _______________**	**Details:- Date: ___/___/___** **Location: _______________** **Bird Variant: _______________**
Bird Name: Bee-Eaters	**Bird Name: Bishops**
Identified ☐	Identified ☐
Where seen? On the:	Where seen? On the:
Ground ☐ Plant ☐ Bush ☐ Tree ☐	Ground ☐ Plant ☐ Bush ☐ Tree ☐
Flying ☐ Dead ☐	Flying ☐ Dead ☐
Male ☐ Female ☐ Adult ☐ Chick ☐	Male ☐ Female ☐ Adult ☐ Chick ☐
Details:- Date: ___/___/___ **Location:** **_______________ Bird** **Variant: _______________**	**Details:- Date: ___/___/___** **Location: _______________** **Bird Variant: _______________**

Bird Name: Bitterns	**Bird Name: Bulbuls**
Identified ☐	Identified ☐
Where seen? On the:	Where seen? On the:
Ground ☐ Plant ☐ Bush ☐ Tree ☐	Ground ☐ Plant ☐ Bush ☐ Tree ☐
Flying ☐ Dead ☐	Flying ☐ Dead ☐
Male ☐ Female ☐ Adult ☐ Chick ☐	Male ☐ Female ☐ Adult ☐ Chick ☐
Details:- Date: ___/___/___ **Location: ____________________** **Bird Variant: _________________**	**Details:- Date: ___/___/___** **Location: ____________________** **Bird Variant: _________________**
Bird Name: Buntings	**Bird Name: Bush Warbler**
Identified ☐	Identified ☐
Where seen? On the:	Where seen? On the:
Ground ☐ Plant ☐ Bush ☐ Tree ☐	Ground ☐ Plant ☐ Bush ☐ Tree ☐
Flying ☐ Dead ☐	Flying ☐ Dead ☐
Male ☐ Female ☐ Adult ☐ Chick ☐	Male ☐ Female ☐ Adult ☐ Chick ☐
Details:- Date: ___/___/___ **Location: ____________________** **Bird Variant: _________________**	**Details:- Date: ___/___/___** **Location: ____________________** **Bird Variant: _________________**
Bird Name: Bustards	**Bird Name: Buzzards**
Identified ☐	Identified ☐
Where seen? On the:	Where seen? On the:
Ground ☐ Plant ☐ Bush ☐ Tree ☐	Ground ☐ Plant ☐ Bush ☐ Tree ☐
Flying ☐ Dead ☐	Flying ☐ Dead ☐
Male ☐ Female ☐ Adult ☐ Chick ☐	Male ☐ Female ☐ Adult ☐ Chick ☐
Details:- Date: ___/___/___ **Location: ____________________** **Bird Variant: _________________**	**Details:- Date: ___/___/___** **Location: ____________________** **Bird Variant: _________________**

Bird Name: Cardinals	**Bird Name: Chats**
Identified ☐	Identified ☐
Where seen? On the:	Where seen? On the:
Ground ☐ Plant ☐ Bush ☐ Tree ☐	Ground ☐ Plant ☐ Bush ☐ Tree ☐
Flying ☐ Dead ☐	Flying ☐ Dead ☐
Male ☐ Female ☐ Adult ☐ Chick ☐	Male ☐ Female ☐ Adult ☐ Chick ☐
Details:- Date: ___/___/___ **Location: ___________________** **Bird Variant: ___________________**	**Details:- Date: ___/___/___** **Location: ___________________** **Bird Variant: ___________________**
Bird Name: Cisticolas	**Bird Name: Coots**
Identified ☐	Identified ☐
Where seen? On the:	Where seen? On the:
Ground ☐ Plant ☐ Bush ☐ Tree ☐	Ground ☐ Plant ☐ Bush ☐ Tree ☐
Flying ☐ Dead ☐	Flying ☐ Dead ☐
Male ☐ Female ☐ Adult ☐ Chick ☐	Male ☐ Female ☐ Adult ☐ Chick ☐
Details:- Date: ___/___/___ **Location: ___________________** **Bird Variant: ___________________**	**Details:- Date: ___/___/___** **Location: ___________________** **Bird Variant: ___________________**
Bird Name: Cormorants	**Bird Name: Coucals**
Identified ☐	Identified ☐
Where seen? On the:	Where seen? On the:
Ground ☐ Plant ☐ Bush ☐ Tree ☐	Ground ☐ Plant ☐ Bush ☐ Tree ☐
Flying ☐ Dead ☐	Flying ☐ Dead ☐
Male ☐ Female ☐ Adult ☐ Chick ☐	Male ☐ Female ☐ Adult ☐ Chick ☐
Details:- Date: ___/___/___ **Location: ___________________** **Bird Variant: ___________________**	**Details:- Date: ___/___/___** **Location: ___________________** **Bird Variant: ___________________**

Bird Name: Coursers	**Bird Name: Crakes**
Identified ☐	Identified ☐
Where seen? On the:	Where seen? On the:
Ground ☐ Plant ☐ Bush ☐ Tree ☐	Ground ☐ Plant ☐ Bush ☐ Tree ☐
Flying ☐ Dead ☐	Flying ☐ Dead ☐
Male ☐ Female ☐ Adult ☐ Chick ☐	Male ☐ Female ☐ Adult ☐ Chick ☐
Details:- Date: ___/___/___ **Location: _______________________** **Bird Variant: _______________________**	**Details:- Date: ___/___/___** **Location: _______________________** **Bird Variant: _______________________**
Bird Name: Cranes	**Bird Name: Creepers**
Identified ☐	Identified ☐
Where seen? On the:	Where seen? On the:
Ground ☐ Plant ☐ Bush ☐ Tree ☐	Ground ☐ Plant ☐ Bush ☐ Tree ☐
Flying ☐ Dead ☐	Flying ☐ Dead ☐
Male ☐ Female ☐ Adult ☐ Chick ☐	Male ☐ Female ☐ Adult ☐ Chick ☐
Details:- Date: ___/___/___ **Location: _______________________** **Bird Variant: _______________________**	**Details:- Date: ___/___/___** **Location: _______________________** **Bird Variant: _______________________**
Bird Name: Crows	**Bird Name: Cuckoos**
Identified ☐	Identified ☐
Where seen? On the:	Where seen? On the:
Ground ☐ Plant ☐ Bush ☐ Tree ☐	Ground ☐ Plant ☐ Bush ☐ Tree ☐
Flying ☐ Dead ☐	Flying ☐ Dead ☐
Male ☐ Female ☐ Adult ☐ Chick ☐	Male ☐ Female ☐ Adult ☐ Chick ☐
Details:- Date: ___/___/___ **Location: _______________________** **Bird Variant: _______________________**	**Details:- Date: ___/___/___** **Location: _______________________** **Bird Variant: _______________________**

Bird Name: Curlews	**Bird Name: Daters**
Identified ☐	Identified ☐
Where seen? On the:	Where seen? On the:
Ground ☐ Plant ☐ Bush ☐ Tree ☐	Ground ☐ Plant ☐ Bush ☐ Tree ☐
Flying ☐ Dead ☐	Flying ☐ Dead ☐
Male ☐ Female ☐ Adult ☐ Chick ☐	Male ☐ Female ☐ Adult ☐ Chick ☐
Details:- Date: ___/___/___ **Location: ______________________** **Bird Variant: ______________________**	**Details:- Date: ___/___/___** **Location: ______________________** **Bird Variant: ______________________**
Bird Name: Dippers	**Bird Name: Divers**
Identified ☐	Identified ☐
Where seen? On the:	Where seen? On the:
Ground ☐ Plant ☐ Bush ☐ Tree ☐	Ground ☐ Plant ☐ Bush ☐ Tree ☐
Flying ☐ Dead ☐	Flying ☐ Dead ☐
Male ☐ Female ☐ Adult ☐ Chick ☐	Male ☐ Female ☐ Adult ☐ Chick ☐
Details:- Date: ___/___/___ **Location: ______________________** **Bird Variant: ______________________**	**Details:- Date: ___/___/___** **Location: ______________________** **Bird Variant: ______________________**
Bird Name: Doves	**Bird Name: Drongoes**
Identified ☐	Identified ☐
Where seen? On the:	Where seen? On the:
Ground ☐ Plant ☐ Bush ☐ Tree ☐	Ground ☐ Plant ☐ Bush ☐ Tree ☐
Flying ☐ Dead ☐	Flying ☐ Dead ☐
Male ☐ Female ☐ Adult ☐ Chick ☐	Male ☐ Female ☐ Adult ☐ Chick ☐
Details:- Date: ___/___/___ **Location: ______________________** **Bird Variant: ______________________**	**Details:- Date: ___/___/___** **Location: ______________________** **Bird Variant: ______________________**

Bird Name: Ducks	**Bird Name: Eagles**
Identified □	Identified □
Where seen? On the:	Where seen? On the:
Ground □ Plant □ Bush □ Tree □	Ground □ Plant □ Bush □ Tree □
Flying □ Dead □	Flying □ Dead □
Male □ Female □ Adult □ Chick □	Male □ Female □ Adult □ Chick □
Details:- Date: ___/___/___ **Location: ______________________** **Bird Variant: ___________________**	**Details:- Date: ___/___/___** **Location: ______________________** **Bird Variant: ___________________**
Bird Name: Egrets	**Bird Name: Estrilids**
Identified □	Identified □
Where seen? On the:	Where seen? On the:
Ground □ Plant □ Bush □ Tree □	Ground □ Plant □ Bush □ Tree □
Flying □ Dead □	Flying □ Dead □
Male □ Female □ Adult □ Chick □	Male □ Female □ Adult □ Chick □
Details:- Date: ___/___/___ **Location: ______________________** **Bird Variant: ___________________**	**Details:- Date: ___/___/___** **Location: ______________________** **Bird Variant: ___________________**
Bird Name: Falcons	**Bird Name: Finches**
Identified □	Identified □
Where seen? On the:	Where seen? On the:
Ground □ Plant □ Bush □ Tree □	Ground □ Plant □ Bush □ Tree □
Flying □ Dead □	Flying □ Dead □
Male □ Female □ Adult □ Chick □	Male □ Female □ Adult □ Chick □
Details:- Date: ___/___/___ **Location: ______________________** **Bird Variant: ___________________**	**Details:- Date: ___/___/___** **Location: ______________________** **Bird Variant: ___________________**

Bird Name: Finfoot	**Bird Name: Flamingos**
Identified ☐	Identified ☐
Where seen? On the:	Where seen? On the:
Ground ☐ Plant ☐ Bush ☐ Tree ☐	Ground ☐ Plant ☐ Bush ☐ Tree ☐
Flying ☐ Dead ☐	Flying ☐ Dead ☐
Male ☐ Female ☐ Adult ☐ Chick ☐	Male ☐ Female ☐ Adult ☐ Chick ☐
Details:- Date: ___/___/___ **Location: ____________________** **Bird Variant: ________________**	**Details:- Date: ___/___/___** **Location: ____________________** **Bird Variant: __________________**
Bird Name: Flycatchers	**Bird Name: Francolins**
Identified ☐	Identified ☐
Where seen? On the:	Where seen? On the:
Ground ☐ Plant ☐ Bush ☐ Tree ☐	Ground ☐ Plant ☐ Bush ☐ Tree ☐
Flying ☐ Dead ☐	Flying ☐ Dead ☐
Male ☐ Female ☐ Adult ☐ Chick ☐	Male ☐ Female ☐ Adult ☐ Chick ☐
Details:- Date: ___/___/___ **Location: ____________________** **Bird Variant: ________________**	**Details:- Date: ___/___/___** **Location: ____________________** **Bird Variant: __________________**
Bird Name: Frigatebirds	**Bird Name: Gallinules**
Identified ☐	Identified ☐
Where seen? On the:	Where seen? On the:
Ground ☐ Plant ☐ Bush ☐ Tree ☐	Ground ☐ Plant ☐ Bush ☐ Tree ☐
Flying ☐ Dead ☐	Flying ☐ Dead ☐
Male ☐ Female ☐ Adult ☐ Chick ☐	Male ☐ Female ☐ Adult ☐ Chick ☐
Details:- Date: ___/___/___ **Location: ____________________** **Bird Variant: ________________**	**Details:- Date: ___/___/___** **Location: ____________________** **Bird Variant: __________________**

Bird Name: Gannets	**Bird Name: Geese**
Identified ☐	Identified ☐
Where seen? On the:	Where seen? On the:
Ground ☐ Plant ☐ Bush ☐ Tree ☐	Ground ☐ Plant ☐ Bush ☐ Tree ☐
Flying ☐ Dead ☐	Flying ☐ Dead ☐
Male ☐ Female ☐ Adult ☐ Chick ☐	Male ☐ Female ☐ Adult ☐ Chick ☐
Details:- Date: ___/___/___ **Location: ______________________** **Bird Variant: ______________________**	**Details:- Date: ___/___/___** **Location: ______________________** **Bird Variant: ______________________**
Bird Name: Godwits	**Bird Name: Grasshopper Warblers**
Identified ☐	Identified ☐
Where seen? On the:	Where seen? On the:
Ground ☐ Plant ☐ Bush ☐ Tree ☐	Ground ☐ Plant ☐ Bush ☐ Tree ☐
Flying ☐ Dead ☐	Flying ☐ Dead ☐
Male ☐ Female ☐ Adult ☐ Chick ☐	Male ☐ Female ☐ Adult ☐ Chick ☐
Details:- Date: ___/___/___ **Location: ______________________** **Bird Variant: ______________________**	**Details:- Date: ___/___/___** **Location: ______________________** **Bird Variant: ______________________**
Bird Name: Grebes	**Bird Name: Greenbuls**
Identified ☐	Identified ☐
Where seen? On the:	Where seen? On the:
Ground ☐ Plant ☐ Bush ☐ Tree ☐	Ground ☐ Plant ☐ Bush ☐ Tree ☐
Flying ☐ Dead ☐	Flying ☐ Dead ☐
Male ☐ Female ☐ Adult ☐ Chick ☐	Male ☐ Female ☐ Adult ☐ Chick ☐
Details:- Date: ___/___/___ **Location: ______________________** **Bird Variant: ______________________**	**Details:- Date: ___/___/___** **Location: ______________________** **Bird Variant: ______________________**

Bird Name: Grouses	**Bird Name: Guineafowl**
Identified ☐	Identified ☐
Where seen? On the:	Where seen? On the:
Ground ☐ Plant ☐ Bush ☐ Tree ☐	Ground ☐ Plant ☐ Bush ☐ Tree ☐
Flying ☐ Dead ☐	Flying ☐ Dead ☐
Male ☐ Female ☐ Adult ☐ Chick ☐	Male ☐ Female ☐ Adult ☐ Chick ☐
Details:- Date: ___/___/___ **Location: ___________________** **Bird Variant: _________________**	**Details:- Date: ___/___/___** **Location: ___________________** **Bird Variant: _________________**
Bird Name: Gulls	**Bird Name: Hammerkop**
Identified ☐	Identified ☐
Where seen? On the:	Where seen? On the:
Ground ☐ Plant ☐ Bush ☐ Tree ☐	Ground ☐ Plant ☐ Bush ☐ Tree ☐
Flying ☐ Dead ☐	Flying ☐ Dead ☐
Male ☐ Female ☐ Adult ☐ Chick ☐	Male ☐ Female ☐ Adult ☐ Chick ☐
Details:- Date: ___/___/___ **Location: ___________________** **Bird Variant: _________________**	**Details:- Date: ___/___/___** **Location: ___________________** **Bird Variant: _________________**
Bird Name: Harriers	**Bird Name: Hawks**
Identified ☐	Identified ☐
Where seen? On the:	Where seen? On the:
Ground ☐ Plant ☐ Bush ☐ Tree ☐	Ground ☐ Plant ☐ Bush ☐ Tree ☐
Flying ☐ Dead ☐	Flying ☐ Dead ☐
Male ☐ Female ☐ Adult ☐ Chick ☐	Male ☐ Female ☐ Adult ☐ Chick ☐
Details:- Date: ___/___/___ **Location: ___________________** **Bird Variant: _________________**	**Details:- Date: ___/___/___** **Location: ___________________** **Bird Variant: _________________**

Bird Name: Heron	Bird Name: Honeyguides
Identified ☐	Identified ☐
Where seen? On the:	Where seen? On the:
Ground ☐ Plant ☐ Bush ☐ Tree ☐	Ground ☐ Plant ☐ Bush ☐ Tree ☐
Flying ☐ Dead ☐	Flying ☐ Dead ☐
Male ☐ Female ☐ Adult ☐ Chick ☐	Male ☐ Female ☐ Adult ☐ Chick ☐
Details:- Date: ___/___/___ **Location: _________________________** **Bird Variant: ______________________**	**Details:- Date: ___/___/___** **Location: _________________________** **Bird Variant: ______________________**
Bird Name: Hoopoes	Bird Name: Hornbills
Identified ☐	Identified ☐
Where seen? On the:	Where seen? On the:
Ground ☐ Plant ☐ Bush ☐ Tree ☐	Ground ☐ Plant ☐ Bush ☐ Tree ☐
Flying ☐ Dead ☐	Flying ☐ Dead ☐
Male ☐ Female ☐ Adult ☐ Chick ☐	Male ☐ Female ☐ Adult ☐ Chick ☐
Details:- Date: ___/___/___ **Location: _________________________** **Bird Variant: ______________________**	**Details:- Date: ___/___/___** **Location: _________________________** **Bird Variant: ______________________**
Bird Name: Ibises	Bird Name: Icterids
Identified ☐	Identified ☐
Where seen? On the:	Where seen? On the:
Ground ☐ Plant ☐ Bush ☐ Tree ☐	Ground ☐ Plant ☐ Bush ☐ Tree ☐
Flying ☐ Dead ☐	Flying ☐ Dead ☐
Male ☐ Female ☐ Adult ☐ Chick ☐	Male ☐ Female ☐ Adult ☐ Chick ☐
Details:- Date: ___/___/___ **Location: _________________________** **Bird Variant: ______________________**	**Details:- Date: ___/___/___** **Location: _________________________** **Bird Variant: ______________________**

Bird Name: Illadopses	**Bird Name: Indigobirds**
Identified □	Identified □
Where seen? On the:	Where seen? On the:
Ground □ Plant □ Bush □ Tree □	Ground □ Plant □ Bush □ Tree □
Flying □ Dead □	Flying □ Dead □
Male □ Female □ Adult □ Chick □	Male □ Female □ Adult □ Chick □
Details:- Date: ___/___/___ **Location: _______________________** **Bird Variant: _______________________**	**Details:- Date: ___/___/___** **Location: _______________________** **Bird Variant: _______________________**
Bird Name: Jacana	**Bird Name: Kingfishers**
Identified □	Identified □
Where seen? On the:	Where seen? On the:
Ground □ Plant □ Bush □ Tree □	Ground □ Plant □ Bush □ Tree □
Flying □ Dead □	Flying □ Dead □
Male □ Female □ Adult □ Chick □	Male □ Female □ Adult □ Chick □
Details:- Date: ___/___/___ **Location: _______________________** **Bird Variant: _______________________**	**Details:- Date: ___/___/___** **Location: _______________________** **Bird Variant: _______________________**
Bird Name: Kinglets	**Bird Name: Kites**
Identified □	Identified □
Where seen? On the:	Where seen? On the:
Ground □ Plant □ Bush □ Tree □	Ground □ Plant □ Bush □ Tree □
Flying □ Dead □	Flying □ Dead □
Male □ Female □ Adult □ Chick □	Male □ Female □ Adult □ Chick □
Details:- Date: ___/___/___ **Location: _______________________** **Bird Variant: _______________________**	**Details:- Date: ___/___/___** **Location: _______________________** **Bird Variant: _______________________**

Bird Name: Lapwings	**Bird Name: Larks**
Identified ☐	Identified ☐
Where seen? On the:	Where seen? On the:
Ground ☐ Plant ☐ Bush ☐ Tree ☐	Ground ☐ Plant ☐ Bush ☐ Tree ☐
Flying ☐ Dead ☐	Flying ☐ Dead ☐
Male ☐ Female ☐ Adult ☐ Chick ☐	Male ☐ Female ☐ Adult ☐ Chick ☐
Details:- Date: ___/___/___ **Location: ____________________** **Bird Variant: __________________**	**Details:- Date: ___/___/___** **Location: ____________________** **Bird Variant: __________________**
Bird Name: Leaf Warblers	**Bird Name: Long-Tailed Tits**
Identified ☐	Identified ☐
Where seen? On the:	Where seen? On the:
Ground ☐ Plant ☐ Bush ☐ Tree ☐	Ground ☐ Plant ☐ Bush ☐ Tree ☐
Flying ☐ Dead ☐	Flying ☐ Dead ☐
Male ☐ Female ☐ Adult ☐ Chick ☐	Male ☐ Female ☐ Adult ☐ Chick ☐
Details:- Date: ___/___/___ **Location: ____________________** **Bird Variant: __________________**	**Details:- Date: ___/___/___** **Location: ____________________** **Bird Variant: __________________**
Bird Name: Longclaws	**Bird Name: Longspurs**
Identified ☐	Identified ☐
Where seen? On the:	Where seen? On the:
Ground ☐ Plant ☐ Bush ☐ Tree ☐	Ground ☐ Plant ☐ Bush ☐ Tree ☐
Flying ☐ Dead ☐	Flying ☐ Dead ☐
Male ☐ Female ☐ Adult ☐ Chick ☐	Male ☐ Female ☐ Adult ☐ Chick ☐
Details:- Date: ___/___/___ **Location: ____________________** **Bird Variant: __________________**	**Details:- Date: ___/___/___** **Location: ____________________** **Bird Variant: __________________**

Bird Name: Martins	**Bird Name: Mockingbirds**
Identified ☐	Identified ☐
Where seen? On the:	Where seen? On the:
Ground ☐ Plant ☐ Bush ☐ Tree ☐	Ground ☐ Plant ☐ Bush ☐ Tree ☐
Flying ☐ Dead ☐	Flying ☐ Dead ☐
Male ☐ Female ☐ Adult ☐ Chick ☐	Male ☐ Female ☐ Adult ☐ Chick ☐
Details:- Date: ___/___/___ **Location: ______________________** **Bird Variant: ____________________**	**Details:- Date: ___/___/___** **Location: ______________________** **Bird Variant: ____________________**
Bird Name: Mousebirds	**Bird Name: New World Warblers**
Identified ☐	Identified ☐
Where seen? On the:	Where seen? On the:
Ground ☐ Plant ☐ Bush ☐ Tree ☐	Ground ☐ Plant ☐ Bush ☐ Tree ☐
Flying ☐ Dead ☐	Flying ☐ Dead ☐
Male ☐ Female ☐ Adult ☐ Chick ☐	Male ☐ Female ☐ Adult ☐ Chick ☐
Details:- Date: ___/___/___ **Location: ______________________** **Bird Variant: ____________________**	**Details:- Date: ___/___/___** **Location: ______________________** **Bird Variant: ____________________**
Bird Name: Nightjars	**Bird Name: Nuthatches**
Identified ☐	Identified ☐
Where seen? On the:	Where seen? On the:
Ground ☐ Plant ☐ Bush ☐ Tree ☐	Ground ☐ Plant ☐ Bush ☐ Tree ☐
Flying ☐ Dead ☐	Flying ☐ Dead ☐
Male ☐ Female ☐ Adult ☐ Chick ☐	Male ☐ Female ☐ Adult ☐ Chick ☐
Details:- Date: ___/___/___ **Location: ______________________** **Bird Variant: ____________________**	**Details:- Date: ___/___/___** **Location: ______________________** **Bird Variant: ____________________**

Bird Name: Orioles	Bird Name: Osprey
Identified ☐	Identified ☐
Where seen? On the:	Where seen? On the:
Ground ☐ Plant ☐ Bush ☐ Tree ☐	Ground ☐ Plant ☐ Bush ☐ Tree ☐
Flying ☐ Dead ☐	Flying ☐ Dead ☐
Male ☐ Female ☐ Adult ☐ Chick ☐	Male ☐ Female ☐ Adult ☐ Chick ☐
Details:- Date: ___/___/___ **Location: _____________________** **Bird Variant: _____________________**	**Details:- Date: ___/___/___** **Location: _____________________** **Bird Variant: _____________________**
Bird Name: Owls	**Bird Name: Oystercatchers**
Identified ☐	Identified ☐
Where seen? On the:	Where seen? On the:
Ground ☐ Plant ☐ Bush ☐ Tree ☐	Ground ☐ Plant ☐ Bush ☐ Tree ☐
Flying ☐ Dead ☐	Flying ☐ Dead ☐
Male ☐ Female ☐ Adult ☐ Chick ☐	Male ☐ Female ☐ Adult ☐ Chick ☐
Details:- Date: ___/___/___ **Location: _____________________** **Bird Variant: _____________________**	**Details:- Date: ___/___/___** **Location: _____________________** **Bird Variant: _____________________**
Bird Name: Parrots	**Bird Name: Partridges**
Identified ☐	Identified ☐
Where seen? On the:	Where seen? On the:
Ground ☐ Plant ☐ Bush ☐ Tree ☐	Ground ☐ Plant ☐ Bush ☐ Tree ☐
Flying ☐ Dead ☐	Flying ☐ Dead ☐
Male ☐ Female ☐ Adult ☐ Chick ☐	Male ☐ Female ☐ Adult ☐ Chick ☐
Details:- Date: ___/___/___ **Location: _____________________** **Bird Variant: _____________________**	**Details:- Date: ___/___/___** **Location: _____________________** **Bird Variant: _____________________**

Bird Name: Pelicans	**Bird Name: Penduline Tits**
Identified ☐	Identified ☐
Where seen? On the:	Where seen? On the:
Ground ☐ Plant ☐ Bush ☐ Tree ☐	Ground ☐ Plant ☐ Bush ☐ Tree ☐
Flying ☐ Dead ☐	Flying ☐ Dead ☐
Male ☐ Female ☐ Adult ☐ Chick ☐	Male ☐ Female ☐ Adult ☐ Chick ☐
Details:- Date: ___/___/___ **Location: _____________________** **Bird Variant: __________________**	**Details:- Date: ___/___/___** **Location: _____________________** **Bird Variant: __________________**
Bird Name: Petrels	**Bird Name: Pheasants**
Identified ☐	Identified ☐
Where seen? On the:	Where seen? On the:
Ground ☐ Plant ☐ Bush ☐ Tree ☐	Ground ☐ Plant ☐ Bush ☐ Tree ☐
Flying ☐ Dead ☐	Flying ☐ Dead ☐
Male ☐ Female ☐ Adult ☐ Chick ☐	Male ☐ Female ☐ Adult ☐ Chick ☐
Details:- Date: ___/___/___ **Location: _____________________** **Bird Variant: __________________**	**Details:- Date: ___/___/___** **Location: _____________________** **Bird Variant: __________________**
Bird Name: Piapacs	**Bird Name: Pigeons**
Identified ☐	Identified ☐
Where seen? On the:	Where seen? On the:
Ground ☐ Plant ☐ Bush ☐ Tree ☐	Ground ☐ Plant ☐ Bush ☐ Tree ☐
Flying ☐ Dead ☐	Flying ☐ Dead ☐
Male ☐ Female ☐ Adult ☐ Chick ☐	Male ☐ Female ☐ Adult ☐ Chick ☐
Details:- Date: ___/___/___ **Location: _____________________** **Bird Variant: __________________**	**Details:- Date: ___/___/___** **Location: _____________________** **Bird Variant: __________________**

Bird Name: Pipits	**Bird Name: Plovers**
Identified ☐	Identified ☐
Where seen? On the:	Where seen? On the:
Ground ☐ Plant ☐ Bush ☐ Tree ☐	Ground ☐ Plant ☐ Bush ☐ Tree ☐
Flying ☐ Dead ☐	Flying ☐ Dead ☐
Male ☐ Female ☐ Adult ☐ Chick ☐	Male ☐ Female ☐ Adult ☐ Chick ☐
Details:- Date: ___/___/___ **Location: _____________________** **Bird Variant: _____________________**	**Details:- Date: ___/___/___** **Location: _____________________** **Bird Variant: _____________________**
Bird Name: Pratincoles	**Bird Name: Quails**
Identified ☐	Identified ☐
Where seen? On the:	Where seen? On the:
Ground ☐ Plant ☐ Bush ☐ Tree ☐	Ground ☐ Plant ☐ Bush ☐ Tree ☐
Flying ☐ Dead ☐	Flying ☐ Dead ☐
Male ☐ Female ☐ Adult ☐ Chick ☐	Male ☐ Female ☐ Adult ☐ Chick ☐
Details:- Date: ___/___/___ **Location: _____________________** **Bird Variant: _____________________**	**Details:- Date: ___/___/___** **Location: _____________________** **Bird Variant: _____________________**
Bird Name: Queleas	**Bird Name: Rails**
Identified ☐	Identified ☐
Where seen? On the:	Where seen? On the:
Ground ☐ Plant ☐ Bush ☐ Tree ☐	Ground ☐ Plant ☐ Bush ☐ Tree ☐
Flying ☐ Dead ☐	Flying ☐ Dead ☐
Male ☐ Female ☐ Adult ☐ Chick ☐	Male ☐ Female ☐ Adult ☐ Chick ☐
Details:- Date: ___/___/___ **Location: _____________________** **Bird Variant: _____________________**	**Details:- Date: ___/___/___** **Location: _____________________** **Bird Variant: _____________________**

Bird Name: Reed Warblers	**Bird Name: Rollers**
Identified ☐	Identified ☐
Where seen? On the:	Where seen? On the:
Ground ☐ Plant ☐ Bush ☐ Tree ☐	Ground ☐ Plant ☐ Bush ☐ Tree ☐
Flying ☐ Dead ☐	Flying ☐ Dead ☐
Male ☐ Female ☐ Adult ☐ Chick ☐	Male ☐ Female ☐ Adult ☐ Chick ☐
Details:- Date: ___/___/___ **Location: ____________________** **Bird Variant: __________________**	**Details:- Date: ___/___/___** **Location: ____________________** **Bird Variant: __________________**
Bird Name: Sandgrouses	**Bird Name: Sandpipers**
Identified ☐	Identified ☐
Where seen? On the:	Where seen? On the:
Ground ☐ Plant ☐ Bush ☐ Tree ☐	Ground ☐ Plant ☐ Bush ☐ Tree ☐
Flying ☐ Dead ☐	Flying ☐ Dead ☐
Male ☐ Female ☐ Adult ☐ Chick ☐	Male ☐ Female ☐ Adult ☐ Chick ☐
Details:- Date: ___/___/___ **Location: ____________________** **Bird Variant: __________________**	**Details:- Date: ___/___/___** **Location: ____________________** **Bird Variant: __________________**
Bird Name: Shearwaters	**Bird Name: Shrikes**
Identified ☐	Identified ☐
Where seen? On the:	Where seen? On the:
Ground ☐ Plant ☐ Bush ☐ Tree ☐	Ground ☐ Plant ☐ Bush ☐ Tree ☐
Flying ☐ Dead ☐	Flying ☐ Dead ☐
Male ☐ Female ☐ Adult ☐ Chick ☐	Male ☐ Female ☐ Adult ☐ Chick ☐
Details:- Date: ___/___/___ **Location: ____________________** **Bird Variant: __________________**	**Details:- Date: ___/___/___** **Location: ____________________** **Bird Variant: __________________**

Bird Name: Skimmers	**Bird Name: Skuas**
Identified ☐	Identified ☐
Where seen? On the:	Where seen? On the:
Ground ☐ Plant ☐ Bush ☐ Tree ☐	Ground ☐ Plant ☐ Bush ☐ Tree ☐
Flying ☐ Dead ☐	Flying ☐ Dead ☐
Male ☐ Female ☐ Adult ☐ Chick ☐	Male ☐ Female ☐ Adult ☐ Chick ☐
Details:- Date: ___/___/___ **Location: ______________________** **Bird Variant: ______________________**	**Details:- Date: ___/___/___** **Location: ______________________** **Bird Variant: ______________________**
Bird Name: Snipes	**Bird Name: Sparrows**
Identified ☐	Identified ☐
Where seen? On the:	Where seen? On the:
Ground ☐ Plant ☐ Bush ☐ Tree ☐	Ground ☐ Plant ☐ Bush ☐ Tree ☐
Flying ☐ Dead ☐	Flying ☐ Dead ☐
Male ☐ Female ☐ Adult ☐ Chick ☐	Male ☐ Female ☐ Adult ☐ Chick ☐
Details:- Date: ___/___/___ **Location: ______________________** **Bird Variant: ______________________**	**Details:- Date: ___/___/___** **Location: ______________________** **Bird Variant: ______________________**
Bird Name: Spoonbills	**Bird Name: Starlings**
Identified ☐	Identified ☐
Where seen? On the:	Where seen? On the:
Ground ☐ Plant ☐ Bush ☐ Tree ☐	Ground ☐ Plant ☐ Bush ☐ Tree ☐
Flying ☐ Dead ☐	Flying ☐ Dead ☐
Male ☐ Female ☐ Adult ☐ Chick ☐	Male ☐ Female ☐ Adult ☐ Chick ☐
Details:- Date: ___/___/___ **Location: ______________________** **Bird Variant: ______________________**	**Details:- Date: ___/___/___** **Location: ______________________** **Bird Variant: ______________________**

Bird Name: Stilts	**Bird Name: Storks**
Identified ☐	Identified ☐
Where seen? On the:	Where seen? On the:
Ground ☐ Plant ☐ Bush ☐ Tree ☐	Ground ☐ Plant ☐ Bush ☐ Tree ☐
Flying ☐ Dead ☐	Flying ☐ Dead ☐
Male ☐ Female ☐ Adult ☐ Chick ☐	Male ☐ Female ☐ Adult ☐ Chick ☐
Details:- Date: ___/___/___ **Location: _____________________** **Bird Variant: _____________________**	**Details:- Date: ___/___/___** **Location: _____________________** **Bird Variant: _____________________**
Details:- Date: ___/___/___ **Location: _____________________** **Bird Variant: _____________________**	**Details:- Date: ___/___/___** **Location: _____________________** **Bird Variant: _____________________**
Identified ☐	Identified ☐
Where seen? On the:	Where seen? On the:
Ground ☐ Plant ☐ Bush ☐ Tree ☐	Ground ☐ Plant ☐ Bush ☐ Tree ☐
Flying ☐ Dead ☐	Flying ☐ Dead ☐
Male ☐ Female ☐ Adult ☐ Chick ☐	Male ☐ Female ☐ Adult ☐ Chick ☐
Details:- Date: ___/___/___ **Location: _____________________** **Bird Variant: _____________________**	**Details:- Date: ___/___/___** **Location: _____________________** **Bird Variant: _____________________**
Bird Name: Swans	**Bird Name: Swifts**
Identified ☐	Identified ☐
Where seen? On the:	Where seen? On the:
Ground ☐ Plant ☐ Bush ☐ Tree ☐	Ground ☐ Plant ☐ Bush ☐ Tree ☐
Flying ☐ Dead ☐	Flying ☐ Dead ☐
Male ☐ Female ☐ Adult ☐ Chick ☐	Male ☐ Female ☐ Adult ☐ Chick ☐
Details:- Date: ___/___/___ **Location: _____________________** **Bird Variant: _____________________**	**Details:- Date: ___/___/___** **Location: _____________________** **Bird Variant: _____________________**

Bird Name: Terns	Bird Name: Thick-Knees
Identified ☐	Identified ☐
Where seen? On the:	Where seen? On the:
Ground ☐ Plant ☐ Bush ☐ Tree ☐	Ground ☐ Plant ☐ Bush ☐ Tree ☐
Flying ☐ Dead ☐	Flying ☐ Dead ☐
Male ☐ Female ☐ Adult ☐ Chick ☐	Male ☐ Female ☐ Adult ☐ Chick ☐
Details:- Date: ___/___/___ **Location: ___________________** **Bird Variant: ________________**	**Details:- Date: ___/___/___** **Location: ___________________** **Bird Variant: ________________**
Bird Name: Thrushes	Bird Name: Tinkerbirds
Identified ☐	Identified ☐
Where seen? On the:	Where seen? On the:
Ground ☐ Plant ☐ Bush ☐ Tree ☐	Ground ☐ Plant ☐ Bush ☐ Tree ☐
Flying ☐ Dead ☐	Flying ☐ Dead ☐
Male ☐ Female ☐ Adult ☐ Chick ☐	Male ☐ Female ☐ Adult ☐ Chick ☐
Details:- Date: ___/___/___ **Location: ___________________** **Bird Variant: ________________**	**Details:- Date: ___/___/___** **Location: ___________________** **Bird Variant: ________________**
Bird Name:Tits	Bird Name: Treecreepers
Identified ☐	Identified ☐
Where seen? On the:	Where seen? On the:
Ground ☐ Plant ☐ Bush ☐ Tree ☐	Ground ☐ Plant ☐ Bush ☐ Tree ☐
Flying ☐ Dead ☐	Flying ☐ Dead ☐
Male ☐ Female ☐ Adult ☐ Chick ☐	Male ☐ Female ☐ Adult ☐ Chick ☐
Details:- Date: ___/___/___ **Location: ___________________** **Bird Variant: ________________**	**Details:- Date: ___/___/___** **Location: ___________________** **Bird Variant: ________________**

Bird Name: Tropicbirds	Bird Name: Turacos
Identified ☐	Identified ☐
Where seen? On the:	Where seen? On the:
Ground ☐ Plant ☐ Bush ☐ Tree ☐	Ground ☐ Plant ☐ Bush ☐ Tree ☐
Flying ☐ Dead ☐	Flying ☐ Dead ☐
Male ☐ Female ☐ Adult ☐ Chick ☐	Male ☐ Female ☐ Adult ☐ Chick ☐
Details:- Date: ___/___/___ **Location: _______________________** **Bird Variant: ____________________**	**Details:- Date: ___/___/___** **Location: _______________________** **Bird Variant: ____________________**
Bird Name: Vireos	**Bird Name: Vultures**
Identified ☐	Identified ☐
Where seen? On the:	Where seen? On the:
Ground ☐ Plant ☐ Bush ☐ Tree ☐	Ground ☐ Plant ☐ Bush ☐ Tree ☐
Flying ☐ Dead ☐	Flying ☐ Dead ☐
Male ☐ Female ☐ Adult ☐ Chick ☐	Male ☐ Female ☐ Adult ☐ Chick ☐
Details:- Date: ___/___/___ **Location: _______________________** **Bird Variant: ____________________**	**Details:- Date: ___/___/___** **Location: _______________________** **Bird Variant: ____________________**
Bird Name: Waders	**Bird Name: Wagtails**
Identified ☐	Identified ☐
Where seen? On the:	Where seen? On the:
Ground ☐ Plant ☐ Bush ☐ Tree ☐	Ground ☐ Plant ☐ Bush ☐ Tree ☐
Flying ☐ Dead ☐	Flying ☐ Dead ☐
Male ☐ Female ☐ Adult ☐ Chick ☐	Male ☐ Female ☐ Adult ☐ Chick ☐
Details:- Date: ___/___/___ **Location: _______________________** **Bird Variant: ____________________**	**Details:- Date: ___/___/___** **Location: _______________________** **Bird Variant: ____________________**

Bird Name: Wallcreepers	**Bird Name: Warblers**
Identified ☐	Identified ☐
Where seen? On the:	Where seen? On the:
Ground ☐ Plant ☐ Bush ☐ Tree ☐	Ground ☐ Plant ☐ Bush ☐ Tree ☐
Flying ☐ Dead ☐	Flying ☐ Dead ☐
Male ☐ Female ☐ Adult ☐ Chick ☐	Male ☐ Female ☐ Adult ☐ Chick ☐
Details:- Date: ___/___/___ **Location: _____________________** **Bird Variant: _____________________**	**Details:- Date: ___/___/___** **Location: _____________________** **Bird Variant: _____________________**
Bird Name: Waxwings	**Bird Name: Weavers**
Identified ☐	Identified ☐
Where seen? On the:	Where seen? On the:
Ground ☐ Plant ☐ Bush ☐ Tree ☐	Ground ☐ Plant ☐ Bush ☐ Tree ☐
Flying ☐ Dead ☐	Flying ☐ Dead ☐
Male ☐ Female ☐ Adult ☐ Chick ☐	Male ☐ Female ☐ Adult ☐ Chick ☐
Details:- Date: ___/___/___ **Location: _____________________** **Bird Variant: _____________________**	**Details:- Date: ___/___/___** **Location: _____________________** **Bird Variant: _____________________**
Bird Name: Wheatears	**Bird Name: White-Eyes**
Identified ☐	Identified ☐
Where seen? On the:	Where seen? On the:
Ground ☐ Plant ☐ Bush ☐ Tree ☐	Ground ☐ Plant ☐ Bush ☐ Tree ☐
Flying ☐ Dead ☐	Flying ☐ Dead ☐
Male ☐ Female ☐ Adult ☐ Chick ☐	Male ☐ Female ☐ Adult ☐ Chick ☐
Details:- Date: ___/___/___ **Location: _____________________** **Bird Variant: _____________________**	**Details:- Date: ___/___/___** **Location: _____________________** **Bird Variant: _____________________**

Bird Name: Whydahs	**Bird Name: Widowbirds**
Identified ☐	Identified ☐
Where seen? On the:	Where seen? On the:
Ground ☐ Plant ☐ Bush ☐ Tree ☐	Ground ☐ Plant ☐ Bush ☐ Tree ☐
Flying ☐ Dead ☐	Flying ☐ Dead ☐
Male ☐ Female ☐ Adult ☐ Chick ☐	Male ☐ Female ☐ Adult ☐ Chick ☐
Details:- Date: ___/___/___ **Location: ____________________** **Bird Variant: _________________**	**Details:- Date: ___/___/___** **Location: ____________________** **Bird Variant: _________________**
Bird Name: Woodpeckers	**Bird Name: Wrens**
Identified ☐	Identified ☐
Where seen? On the:	Where seen? On the:
Ground ☐ Plant ☐ Bush ☐ Tree ☐	Ground ☐ Plant ☐ Bush ☐ Tree ☐
Flying ☐ Dead ☐	Flying ☐ Dead ☐
Male ☐ Female ☐ Adult ☐ Chick ☐	Male ☐ Female ☐ Adult ☐ Chick ☐
Details:- Date: ___/___/___ **Location: ____________________** **Bird Variant: _________________**	**Details:- Date: ___/___/___** **Location: ____________________** **Bird Variant: _________________**
Bird Name: Wrynecks	**Bird Name:**
Identified ☐	Identified ☐
Where seen? On the:	Where seen? On the:
Ground ☐ Plant ☐ Bush ☐ Tree ☐	Ground ☐ Plant ☐ Bush ☐ Tree ☐
Flying ☐ Dead ☐	Flying ☐ Dead ☐
Male ☐ Female ☐ Adult ☐ Chick ☐	Male ☐ Female ☐ Adult ☐ Chick ☐
Details:- Date: ___/___/___ **Location: ____________________** **Bird Variant: _________________**	**Details:- Date: ___/___/___** **Location: ____________________** **Bird Variant: _________________**

Bird Name:	**Bird Name:**
Identified □	Identified □
Where seen? On the:	Where seen? On the:
Ground □ Plant □ Bush □ Tree □	Ground □ Plant □ Bush □ Tree □
Flying □ Dead □	Flying □ Dead □
Male □ Female □ Adult □ Chick □	Male □ Female □ Adult □ Chick □
Details:- Date: ___/___/___ **Location: ____________________** **Bird Variant: ____________________**	**Details:- Date: ___/___/___** **Location: ____________________** **Bird Variant: ____________________**
Bird Name:	**Bird Name:**
Identified □	Identified □
Where seen? On the:	Where seen? On the:
Ground □ Plant □ Bush □ Tree □	Ground □ Plant □ Bush □ Tree □
Flying □ Dead □	Flying □ Dead □
Male □ Female □ Adult □ Chick □	Male □ Female □ Adult □ Chick □
Details:- Date: ___/___/___ **Location: ____________________** **Bird Variant: ____________________**	**Details:- Date: ___/___/___** **Location: ____________________** **Bird Variant: ____________________**
Bird Name:	**Bird Name:**
Identified □	Identified □
Where seen? On the:	Where seen? On the:
Ground □ Plant □ Bush □ Tree □	Ground □ Plant □ Bush □ Tree □
Flying □ Dead □	Flying □ Dead □
Male □ Female □ Adult □ Chick □	Male □ Female □ Adult □ Chick □
Details:- Date: ___/___/___ **Location: ____________________** **Bird Variant: ____________________**	**Details:- Date: ___/___/___** **Location: ____________________** **Bird Variant: ____________________**

Bird Name:	**Bird Name:**
Identified □	Identified □
Where seen? On the:	Where seen? On the:
Ground □ Plant □ Bush □ Tree □	Ground □ Plant □ Bush □ Tree □
Flying □ Dead □	Flying □ Dead □
Male □ Female □ Adult □ Chick □	Male □ Female □ Adult □ Chick □
Details:- Date: ___/___/___ **Location: ______________________** **Bird Variant: ______________________**	**Details:- Date: ___/___/___** **Location: ______________________** **Bird Variant: ______________________**
Bird Name:	**Bird Name:**
Identified □	Identified □
Where seen? On the:	Where seen? On the:
Ground □ Plant □ Bush □ Tree □	Ground □ Plant □ Bush □ Tree □
Flying □ Dead □	Flying □ Dead □
Male □ Female □ Adult □ Chick □	Male □ Female □ Adult □ Chick □
Details:- Date: ___/___/___ **Location: ______________________** **Bird Variant: ______________________**	**Details:- Date: ___/___/___** **Location: ______________________** **Bird Variant: ______________________**
Bird Name:	**Bird Name:**
Identified □	Identified □
Where seen? On the:	Where seen? On the:
Ground □ Plant □ Bush □ Tree □	Ground □ Plant □ Bush □ Tree □
Flying □ Dead □	Flying □ Dead □
Male □ Female □ Adult □ Chick □	Male □ Female □ Adult □ Chick □
Details:- Date: ___/___/___ **Location: ______________________** **Bird Variant: ______________________**	**Details:- Date: ___/___/___** **Location: ______________________** **Bird Variant: ______________________**

Bird Name:	**Bird Name:**
Identified □	Identified □
Where seen? On the:	Where seen? On the:
Ground □ Plant □ Bush □ Tree □	Ground □ Plant □ Bush □ Tree □
Flying □ Dead □	Flying □ Dead □
Male □ Female □ Adult □ Chick □	Male □ Female □ Adult □ Chick □
Details:- Date: ___/___/___ Location: _________________________ Bird Variant: ____________________	**Details:- Date: ___/___/___ Location: _________________________ Bird Variant: ____________________**
Bird Name:	**Bird Name:**
Identified □	Identified □
Where seen? On the:	Where seen? On the:
Ground □ Plant □ Bush □ Tree □	Ground □ Plant □ Bush □ Tree □
Flying □ Dead □	Flying □ Dead □
Male □ Female □ Adult □ Chick □	Male □ Female □ Adult □ Chick □
Details:- Date: ___/___/___ Location: _________________________ Bird Variant: ____________________	**Details:- Date: ___/___/___ Location: _________________________ Bird Variant: ____________________**
Bird Name:	**Bird Name:**
Identified □	Identified □
Where seen? On the:	Where seen? On the:
Ground □ Plant □ Bush □ Tree □	Ground □ Plant □ Bush □ Tree □
Flying □ Dead □	Flying □ Dead □
Male □ Female □ Adult □ Chick □	Male □ Female □ Adult □ Chick □
Details:- Date: ___/___/___ Location: _________________________ Bird Variant: ____________________	**Details:- Date: ___/___/___ Location: _________________________ Bird Variant: ____________________**

Bird Name:	**Bird Name:**
Identified □	Identified □
Where seen? On the:	Where seen? On the:
Ground □ Plant □ Bush □ Tree □	Ground □ Plant □ Bush □ Tree □
Flying □ Dead □	Flying □ Dead □
Male □ Female □ Adult □ Chick □	Male □ Female □ Adult □ Chick □
Details:- Date: ___/___/___ **Location: ____________________** **Bird Variant: ____________________**	**Details:- Date: ___/___/___** **Location: ____________________** **Bird Variant: ____________________**
Bird Name:	**Bird Name:**
Identified □	Identified □
Where seen? On the:	Where seen? On the:
Ground □ Plant □ Bush □ Tree □	Ground □ Plant □ Bush □ Tree □
Flying □ Dead □	Flying □ Dead □
Male □ Female □ Adult □ Chick □	Male □ Female □ Adult □ Chick □
Details:- Date: ___/___/___ **Location: ____________________** **Bird Variant: ____________________**	**Details:- Date: ___/___/___** **Location: ____________________** **Bird Variant: ____________________**
Bird Name:	**Bird Name:**
Identified □	Identified □
Where seen? On the:	Where seen? On the:
Ground □ Plant □ Bush □ Tree □	Ground □ Plant □ Bush □ Tree □
Flying □ Dead □	Flying □ Dead □
Male □ Female □ Adult □ Chick □	Male □ Female □ Adult □ Chick □
Details:- Date: ___/___/___ **Location: ____________________** **Bird Variant: ____________________**	**Details:- Date: ___/___/___** **Location: ____________________** **Bird Variant: ____________________**

Bird Name:	**Bird Name:**
Identified □	Identified □
Where seen? On the:	Where seen? On the:
Ground □ Plant □ Bush □ Tree □	Ground □ Plant □ Bush □ Tree □
Flying □ Dead □	Flying □ Dead □
Male □ Female □ Adult □ Chick □	Male □ Female □ Adult □ Chick □
Details:- Date: ___/___/___ **Location: ____________________** **Bird Variant: ____________________**	**Details:- Date: ___/___/___** **Location: ____________________** **Bird Variant: ____________________**
Bird Name:	**Bird Name:**
Identified □	Identified □
Where seen? On the:	Where seen? On the:
Ground □ Plant □ Bush □ Tree □	Ground □ Plant □ Bush □ Tree □
Flying □ Dead □	Flying □ Dead □
Male □ Female □ Adult □ Chick □	Male □ Female □ Adult □ Chick □
Details:- Date: ___/___/___ **Location: ____________________** **Bird Variant: ____________________**	**Details:- Date: ___/___/___** **Location: ____________________** **Bird Variant: ____________________**
Bird Name:	**Bird Name:**
Identified □	Identified □
Where seen? On the:	Where seen? On the:
Ground □ Plant □ Bush □ Tree □	Ground □ Plant □ Bush □ Tree □
Flying □ Dead □	Flying □ Dead □
Male □ Female □ Adult □ Chick □	Male □ Female □ Adult □ Chick □
Details:- Date: ___/___/___ **Location: ____________________** **Bird Variant: ____________________**	**Details:- Date: ___/___/___** **Location: ____________________** **Bird Variant: ____________________**

Bird Name:	**Bird Name:**
Identified □	Identified □
Where seen? On the:	Where seen? On the:
Ground □ Plant □ Bush □ Tree □	Ground □ Plant □ Bush □ Tree □
Flying □ Dead □	Flying □ Dead □
Male □ Female □ Adult □ Chick □	Male □ Female □ Adult □ Chick □
Details:- Date: ___/___/___ **Location: _______________________** **Bird Variant: _____________________**	**Details:- Date: ___/___/___** **Location: _______________________** **Bird Variant: _____________________**
Bird Name:	**Bird Name:**
Identified □	Identified □
Where seen? On the:	Where seen? On the:
Ground □ Plant □ Bush □ Tree □	Ground □ Plant □ Bush □ Tree □
Flying □ Dead □	Flying □ Dead □
Male □ Female □ Adult □ Chick □	Male □ Female □ Adult □ Chick □
Details:- Date: ___/___/___ **Location: _______________________** **Bird Variant: _____________________**	**Details:- Date: ___/___/___** **Location: _______________________** **Bird Variant: _____________________**
Bird Name:	**Bird Name:**
Identified □	Identified □
Where seen? On the:	Where seen? On the:
Ground □ Plant □ Bush □ Tree □	Ground □ Plant □ Bush □ Tree □
Flying □ Dead □	Flying □ Dead □
Male □ Female □ Adult □ Chick □	Male □ Female □ Adult □ Chick □
Details:- Date: ___/___/___ **Location: _______________________** **Bird Variant: _____________________**	**Details:- Date: ___/___/___** **Location: _______________________** **Bird Variant: _____________________**

Bird Name:	**Bird Name:**
Identified □	Identified □
Where seen? On the:	Where seen? On the:
Ground □ Plant □ Bush □ Tree □	Ground □ Plant □ Bush □ Tree □
Flying □ Dead □	Flying □ Dead □
Male □ Female □ Adult □ Chick □	Male □ Female □ Adult □ Chick □
Details:- Date: ___/___/___ **Location: _______________________** **Bird Variant: _____________________**	**Details:- Date: ___/___/___** **Location: _______________________** **Bird Variant: _____________________**
Bird Name:	**Bird Name:**
Identified □	Identified □
Where seen? On the:	Where seen? On the:
Ground □ Plant □ Bush □ Tree □	Ground □ Plant □ Bush □ Tree □
Flying □ Dead □	Flying □ Dead □
Male □ Female □ Adult □ Chick □	Male □ Female □ Adult □ Chick □
Details:- Date: ___/___/___ **Location: _______________________** **Bird Variant: _____________________**	**Details:- Date: ___/___/___** **Location: _______________________** **Bird Variant: _____________________**
Bird Name:	**Bird Name:**
Identified □	Identified □
Where seen? On the:	Where seen? On the:
Ground □ Plant □ Bush □ Tree □	Ground □ Plant □ Bush □ Tree □
Flying □ Dead □	Flying □ Dead □
Male □ Female □ Adult □ Chick □	Male □ Female □ Adult □ Chick □
Details:- Date: ___/___/___ **Location: _______________________** **Bird Variant: _____________________**	**Details:- Date: ___/___/___** **Location: _______________________** **Bird Variant: _____________________**

Bird Name:	Bird Name:
Identified ☐	Identified ☐
Where seen? On the:	Where seen? On the:
Ground ☐ Plant ☐ Bush ☐ Tree ☐	Ground ☐ Plant ☐ Bush ☐ Tree ☐
Flying ☐ Dead ☐	Flying ☐ Dead ☐
Male ☐ Female ☐ Adult ☐ Chick ☐	Male ☐ Female ☐ Adult ☐ Chick ☐
Details:- Date: ___/___/___ **Location: _____________________** **Bird Variant: _____________________**	**Details:- Date: ___/___/___** **Location: _____________________** **Bird Variant: _____________________**
Bird Name:	**Bird Name:**
Identified ☐	Identified ☐
Where seen? On the:	Where seen? On the:
Ground ☐ Plant ☐ Bush ☐ Tree ☐	Ground ☐ Plant ☐ Bush ☐ Tree ☐
Flying ☐ Dead ☐	Flying ☐ Dead ☐
Male ☐ Female ☐ Adult ☐ Chick ☐	Male ☐ Female ☐ Adult ☐ Chick ☐
Details:- Date: ___/___/___ **Location: _____________________** **Bird Variant: _____________________**	**Details:- Date: ___/___/___** **Location: _____________________** **Bird Variant: _____________________**
Bird Name:	**Bird Name:**
Identified ☐	Identified ☐
Where seen? On the:	Where seen? On the:
Ground ☐ Plant ☐ Bush ☐ Tree ☐	Ground ☐ Plant ☐ Bush ☐ Tree ☐
Flying ☐ Dead ☐	Flying ☐ Dead ☐
Male ☐ Female ☐ Adult ☐ Chick ☐	Male ☐ Female ☐ Adult ☐ Chick ☐
Details:- Date: ___/___/___ **Location: _____________________** **Bird Variant: _____________________**	**Details:- Date: ___/___/___** **Location: _____________________** **Bird Variant: _____________________**

Bird Name:	**Bird Name:**
Identified ☐	Identified ☐
Where seen? On the:	Where seen? On the:
Ground ☐ Plant ☐ Bush ☐ Tree ☐	Ground ☐ Plant ☐ Bush ☐ Tree ☐
Flying ☐ Dead ☐	Flying ☐ Dead ☐
Male ☐ Female ☐ Adult ☐ Chick ☐	Male ☐ Female ☐ Adult ☐ Chick ☐
Details:- Date: ___/___/___ **Location: ______________________** **Bird Variant: ______________________**	**Details:- Date: ___/___/___** **Location: ______________________** **Bird Variant: ______________________**
Bird Name:	**Bird Name:**
Identified ☐	Identified ☐
Where seen? On the:	Where seen? On the:
Ground ☐ Plant ☐ Bush ☐ Tree ☐	Ground ☐ Plant ☐ Bush ☐ Tree ☐
Flying ☐ Dead ☐	Flying ☐ Dead ☐
Male ☐ Female ☐ Adult ☐ Chick ☐	Male ☐ Female ☐ Adult ☐ Chick ☐
Details:- Date: ___/___/___ **Location: ______________________** **Bird Variant: ______________________**	**Details:- Date: ___/___/___** **Location: ______________________** **Bird Variant: ______________________**
Bird Name:	**Bird Name:**
Identified ☐	Identified ☐
Where seen? On the:	Where seen? On the:
Ground ☐ Plant ☐ Bush ☐ Tree ☐	Ground ☐ Plant ☐ Bush ☐ Tree ☐
Flying ☐ Dead ☐	Flying ☐ Dead ☐
Male ☐ Female ☐ Adult ☐ Chick ☐	Male ☐ Female ☐ Adult ☐ Chick ☐
Details:- Date: ___/___/___ **Location: ______________________** **Bird Variant: ______________________**	**Details:- Date: ___/___/___** **Location: ______________________** **Bird Variant: ______________________**

Bird Name:	**Bird Name:**
Identified □	Identified □
Where seen? On the:	Where seen? On the:
Ground □ Plant □ Bush □ Tree □	Ground □ Plant □ Bush □ Tree □
Flying □ Dead □	Flying □ Dead □
Male □ Female □ Adult □ Chick □	Male □ Female □ Adult □ Chick □
Details:- Date: ___/___/___ **Location: ____________________** **Bird Variant: ____________________**	**Details:- Date: ___/___/___** **Location: ____________________** **Bird Variant: ____________________**
Bird Name:	**Bird Name:**
Identified □	Identified □
Where seen? On the:	Where seen? On the:
Ground □ Plant □ Bush □ Tree □	Ground □ Plant □ Bush □ Tree □
Flying □ Dead □	Flying □ Dead □
Male □ Female □ Adult □ Chick □	Male □ Female □ Adult □ Chick □
Details:- Date: ___/___/___ **Location: ____________________** **Bird Variant: ____________________**	**Details:- Date: ___/___/___** **Location: ____________________** **Bird Variant: ____________________**
Bird Name:	**Bird Name:**
Identified □	Identified □
Where seen? On the:	Where seen? On the:
Ground □ Plant □ Bush □ Tree □	Ground □ Plant □ Bush □ Tree □
Flying □ Dead □	Flying □ Dead □
Male □ Female □ Adult □ Chick □	Male □ Female □ Adult □ Chick □
Details:- Date: ___/___/___ **Location: ____________________** **Bird Variant: ____________________**	**Details:- Date: ___/___/___** **Location: ____________________** **Bird Variant: ____________________**

Bird Name:	**Bird Name:**
Identified □	Identified □
Where seen? On the:	Where seen? On the:
Ground □ Plant □ Bush □ Tree □	Ground □ Plant □ Bush □ Tree □
Flying □ Dead □	Flying □ Dead □
Male □ Female □ Adult □ Chick □	Male □ Female □ Adult □ Chick □
Details:- Date: ___/___/___ **Location: _____________________** **Bird Variant: _____________________**	**Details:- Date: ___/___/___** **Location: _____________________** **Bird Variant: _____________________**
Bird Name:	**Bird Name:**
Identified □	Identified □
Where seen? On the:	Where seen? On the:
Ground □ Plant □ Bush □ Tree □	Ground □ Plant □ Bush □ Tree □
Flying □ Dead □	Flying □ Dead □
Male □ Female □ Adult □ Chick □	Male □ Female □ Adult □ Chick □
Details:- Date: ___/___/___ **Location: _____________________** **Bird Variant: _____________________**	**Details:- Date: ___/___/___** **Location: _____________________** **Bird Variant: _____________________**
Bird Name:	**Bird Name:**
Identified □	Identified □
Where seen? On the:	Where seen? On the:
Ground □ Plant □ Bush □ Tree □	Ground □ Plant □ Bush □ Tree □
Flying □ Dead □	Flying □ Dead □
Male □ Female □ Adult □ Chick □	Male □ Female □ Adult □ Chick □
Details:- Date: ___/___/___ **Location: _____________________** **Bird Variant: _____________________**	**Details:- Date: ___/___/___** **Location: _____________________** **Bird Variant: _____________________**

Bird Name:	**Bird Name:**
Identified ☐	Identified ☐
Where seen? On the:	Where seen? On the:
Ground ☐ Plant ☐ Bush ☐ Tree ☐	Ground ☐ Plant ☐ Bush ☐ Tree ☐
Flying ☐ Dead ☐	Flying ☐ Dead ☐
Male ☐ Female ☐ Adult ☐ Chick ☐	Male ☐ Female ☐ Adult ☐ Chick ☐
Details:- Date: ___/___/___ **Location: ______________________** **Bird Variant: ___________________**	**Details:- Date: ___/___/___** **Location: ______________________** **Bird Variant: ___________________**
Bird Name:	**Bird Name:**
Identified ☐	Identified ☐
Where seen? On the:	Where seen? On the:
Ground ☐ Plant ☐ Bush ☐ Tree ☐	Ground ☐ Plant ☐ Bush ☐ Tree ☐
Flying ☐ Dead ☐	Flying ☐ Dead ☐
Male ☐ Female ☐ Adult ☐ Chick ☐	Male ☐ Female ☐ Adult ☐ Chick ☐
Details:- Date: ___/___/___ **Location: ______________________** **Bird Variant: ___________________**	**Details:- Date: ___/___/___** **Location: ______________________** **Bird Variant: ___________________**
Bird Name:	**Bird Name:**
Identified ☐	Identified ☐
Where seen? On the:	Where seen? On the:
Ground ☐ Plant ☐ Bush ☐ Tree ☐	Ground ☐ Plant ☐ Bush ☐ Tree ☐
Flying ☐ Dead ☐	Flying ☐ Dead ☐
Male ☐ Female ☐ Adult ☐ Chick ☐	Male ☐ Female ☐ Adult ☐ Chick ☐
Details:- Date: ___/___/___ **Location: ______________________** **Bird Variant: ___________________**	**Details:- Date: ___/___/___** **Location: ______________________** **Bird Variant: ___________________**

Bird Name:	**Bird Name:**
Identified □	Identified □
Where seen? On the:	Where seen? On the:
Ground □ Plant □ Bush □ Tree □	Ground □ Plant □ Bush □ Tree □
Flying □ Dead □	Flying □ Dead □
Male □ Female □ Adult □ Chick □	Male □ Female □ Adult □ Chick □
Details:- Date: ___/___/___ **Location: _______________________** **Bird Variant: _______________________**	**Details:- Date: ___/___/___** **Location: _______________________** **Bird Variant: _______________________**
Bird Name:	**Bird Name:**
Identified □	Identified □
Where seen? On the:	Where seen? On the:
Ground □ Plant □ Bush □ Tree □	Ground □ Plant □ Bush □ Tree □
Flying □ Dead □	Flying □ Dead □
Male □ Female □ Adult □ Chick □	Male □ Female □ Adult □ Chick □
Details:- Date: ___/___/___ **Location: _______________________** **Bird Variant: _______________________**	**Details:- Date: ___/___/___** **Location: _______________________** **Bird Variant: _______________________**
Bird Name:	**Bird Name:**
Identified □	Identified □
Where seen? On the:	Where seen? On the:
Ground □ Plant □ Bush □ Tree □	Ground □ Plant □ Bush □ Tree □
Flying □ Dead □	Flying □ Dead □
Male □ Female □ Adult □ Chick □	Male □ Female □ Adult □ Chick □
Details:- Date: ___/___/___ **Location: _______________________** **Bird Variant: _______________________**	**Details:- Date: ___/___/___** **Location: _______________________** **Bird Variant: _______________________**

Bird Name:	**Bird Name:**
Identified ☐	Identified ☐
Where seen? On the:	Where seen? On the:
Ground ☐ Plant ☐ Bush ☐ Tree ☐	Ground ☐ Plant ☐ Bush ☐ Tree ☐
Flying ☐ Dead ☐	Flying ☐ Dead ☐
Male ☐ Female ☐ Adult ☐ Chick ☐	Male ☐ Female ☐ Adult ☐ Chick ☐
Details:- Date: ___/___/___ **Location: _______________________** **Bird Variant: _____________________**	**Details:- Date: ___/___/___** **Location: _______________________** **Bird Variant: _____________________**
Bird Name:	**Bird Name:**
Identified ☐	Identified ☐
Where seen? On the:	Where seen? On the:
Ground ☐ Plant ☐ Bush ☐ Tree ☐	Ground ☐ Plant ☐ Bush ☐ Tree ☐
Flying ☐ Dead ☐	Flying ☐ Dead ☐
Male ☐ Female ☐ Adult ☐ Chick ☐	Male ☐ Female ☐ Adult ☐ Chick ☐
Details:- Date: ___/___/___ **Location: _______________________** **Bird Variant: _____________________**	**Details:- Date: ___/___/___** **Location: _______________________** **Bird Variant: _____________________**
Bird Name:	**Bird Name:**
Identified ☐	Identified ☐
Where seen? On the:	Where seen? On the:
Ground ☐ Plant ☐ Bush ☐ Tree ☐	Ground ☐ Plant ☐ Bush ☐ Tree ☐
Flying ☐ Dead ☐	Flying ☐ Dead ☐
Male ☐ Female ☐ Adult ☐ Chick ☐	Male ☐ Female ☐ Adult ☐ Chick ☐
Details:- Date: ___/___/___ **Location: _______________________** **Bird Variant: _____________________**	**Details:- Date: ___/___/___** **Location: _______________________** **Bird Variant: _____________________**